A Keepsake Book from the

HEART OF THE HOME

Sweets to the Sweet

by

Susan Branch

My Book

LITTLE, BROWN AND COMPANY

Boston · New York   Toronto · London

FIRST EDITION

ISBN 0-316-10622-4

Published simultaneously in Canada
by Little, Brown & Company
(Canada) Limited

MANUFACTURED IN CHINA

Contents

The Little Book of Big Desserts

SEE PAGE 4
FOR THE CONTEST-
    WINNING RECIPE

Last year the people at　　　　Little Brown (my publisher since 1986) & I de-　　　　cided we wanted to do some-thing nice for all the people who have bought my books. We thought a recipe contest would be fun — the Grand Prize would be a week-end for 2 on Martha's Vineyard (including round trip!) at a country inn, dinner on the island at the famous Black Dog Tavern; & a visit to my house. So I sent contest brochures to everyone on my News-letter list, & Little Brown put them in the 1998 wall-calen-dars & into new printings of books — they were everywhere! And sud-denly TEN BILLION RECIPES came in (well, probably not ten billion) but recipes GALORE. And they looked soooo good; you could gain weight reading them. Since I was supposed to be home painting the 1999 calendar, Little Brown promised to do the testing. They cooked & baked, whittled & narrowed until finally, after weeks they selected their "Top Ten" which they turned over to me. That is when I partially began to understand what they'd gone through. Be-cause every single recipe was a pearl & now I had to choose one. It was hard! Everyone deserved to win! But that's not the way it works. So folks, we HAVE our winner! Her name is Vita Wayne of Hicksville, New York, for "Fairy Cakes". She entered with the blessings of the actual author of this ethereal concoction, her "feisty, witty, exuberant" 91 year old neighbor Margherita Avila (mother of Vita's best friend Pat who'll be coming with Vita to the Vineyard. ♥)

　　　　I loved talking to Vita on the phone — it was fun telling her she'd won — & I look forward to our Mother's Day visit on the island. And from the bottom of my heart, I thank you all for your enthusiastic participation, great recipes, sweet stories. This was a pure pleasure. Look for the names of the 5 runners-up in my next Newsletter. Till then, enjoy this delicious dessert. ❤

Fairy Cakes

375° Makes 18 large
or 36 small cakes

Whole eggs & fresh milk provide the base for the creamiest custard (cuddled) inside (as a sweet surprise) tender, impossibly light baby cakes. ♥

Cream Filling

4 c. milk (1 qt.)	1/4 c. cornstarch
1/2 c. sugar	4 lg. egg yolks
1 whole lemon . . . . . peel (in one piece)	

Whisk all ingred. together in a saucepan over med. high heat. Stir constantly till thick. Remove lemon rind & set aside to cool. ♥ (note: this makes a lot more than you need to fill the cakes, which I never regretted all 3 times I made it — lots of fun stuff to do with the extra ♥).

Cakes

6 large eggs	2 tsp. baking powder
1 c. sugar	2 tsp. vanilla
1 c. cake flour	confectioners sugar

Preheat oven to 375°. Beat whole eggs & sugar in mixer till well blended. Add flour & continue beating 10 min. Add baking powder & vanilla, beat 5 min. more. Pour into generously greased muffin tins — fill 1/2 to 3/4 full. Bake in the middle of the oven for 10-15 min. till just golden, but not brown. Remove from tins as soon as possible. When slightly cooled, partially cut off tops of cakes, pull out a little "plug" of cake from bottom half & fill with cream. Sift over a little powdered sugar & chill cakes. ♥ Also good with fresh berries, chocolate glaze (p.16) or a spoonful of whipped cream. Plain or gilded, they are wonderful.

-5-

REMEMBER: PIES & CAKES ARE AN IMPORTANT PART OF A BALANCED DIET.

Make someone happy today & bake a big, beautiful cake — a cake for a party, a cake for a friend, a heart-shaped cake for LOVE.

CAKE TIPS

Old-fashioned shiny metal pans are best for a lightly browned, tender cake.

All utensils & ingredients for cake baking (including eggs & milk) should be at room temperature.

Even a few minutes too long in the oven can dry out a cake; check doneness by inserting a clean knife or tooth-pick into center - if it comes out clean, it's done.

Before icing, tuck strips of waxed paper under edges of cake to catch extra frosting — they'll pull out easily when you finish.

Using a pastry bag to decorate is fun — you can write messages, make roses & other flowers, do little borders in rosettes or stars, try latticework. Practice on waxed paper first.

Fresh flowers are beautiful on cakes — rosebuds, a single lily, marigolds or a scattering of wild violets.

My mother used to bake dimes into our birthday cakes — we considered her a genius. Try using sparklers on B'day cakes instead of candles.

6

Happy Baking!

CAKES & PIES

ORANGE CAKE

Serves 8~10

To die for. ♥ A real special-occasion cake perfect for spring teas, Mother's Day, showers or a pre~ wedding party. ♥

Orange Filling

6 Tbsp. sugar	½ tsp. grated orange peel
1½ Tbsp. cornstarch	½ c. fresh orange juice
pinch of salt	1 egg yolk, slightly beaten
½ c. water	1 Tbsp. butter, melted

½ c. crushed pineapple

In top part of double boiler, over boiling water, mix sugar, cornstarch & salt. Gradually add water, orange peel & juice, then egg yolk. Cook, stirring, till smooth & thick. Fold in butter & pineapple. Chill ♥

The Cake

4 Tbsp. butter	1½ c. flour
1 c. sugar	2 tsp. baking powder
2 eggs, separated	pinch of salt

½ c. fresh orange juice

Preheat oven to 350°. Cream butter & sugar. Add egg yolks & beat till thick & lemon-colored. With a fork, mix together dry ingredients & add them alternately with the o.j. Fold in stiffly beaten egg whites. Pour into two buttered 8" cake pans & bake at 350° for 20 minutes. Cool completely & remove from pans. ♥

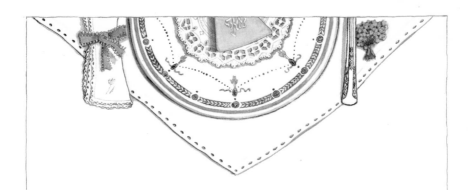

Orange Icing

zest of 1 orange   1½ c. powdered sugar
juice of 1 orange   1 tsp. white rum
            coconut for garnish (opt.)

Lightly grate rind of orange & bring it & the juice to a boil. Strain the juice & pour as much hot juice over sugar as needed to make right consistency for spreading. Stir in rum. ♥

To Assemble

Put the chilled filling between layers. Frost with orange icing, allowing some to dribble over edges. Sprinkle on coconut if you like. The cake looks beautiful served on plates lined with lace doilies. ♥

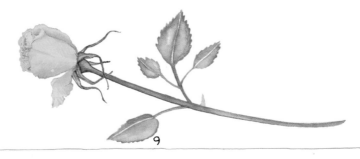

PINEAPPLE UPSIDE-DOWN CAKE
WITH VANILLA SAUCE

350° Serves 8

Try not to drink the sauce; it's perfect with this old-fashioned picnic cake. ♥

3 Tbsp. butter
3/4 c. brown sugar
1 lb. can pineapple rings
walnut halves
3 eggs
1 c. sugar

1/2 c. juice drained from pineapple
1½ tsp. vanilla
1½ c. sifted flour
½ tsp. baking powder
½ tsp. salt

Preheat oven to 350°. Melt 3 Tbsp. butter in a 9" oven-proof skillet, or any straight-sided pan — I use a spring-form. Sprinkle in brown sugar. Arrange pineapple slices (saving the juice) over the sugar — put walnuts in pineapple centers & around edges. Put pan into oven to warm (but don't cook). In a med. bowl beat eggs till fluffy; gradually beat in sugar. Add pineapple syrup & vanilla. Sift flour, baking powder & salt; add all at once & beat smooth. Pour over pineapple. Bake 50 min. Turn out onto cake plate. Looks great decorated with calendulas around the edge — marigolds too. Put a puddle of Vanilla Sauce on a plate — put a slice of cake right smack in the middle of it. Serve. ♥

VANILLA SAUCE

1" piece of vanilla bean
2 c. heavy cream

1/4 c. sugar

Slit vanilla bean in half & scrape pulp into a small saucepan. Stir in cream & bring to a boil. Add sugar, stir & let it cool. Chill well. ♥

THREE-LAYER CARROT CAKE

325°

This cake goes together so easily and it has everything: it's very moist, chock-full of nuts and fruit, and it's tall and gorgeous ~ A perfect Birthday Cake. 🍴

4 eggs, well beaten
1 c. packed brown sugar
1 c. white sugar
1½ c. vegetable oil
2 c. unbleached flour
2 tsp. baking soda
2 tsp. baking powder

2 tsp. cinnamon
1½ tsp. nutmeg
3 c. finely grated carrots
1 c. coconut
1 8 oz. can crushed pineapple
1 c. golden raisins
1 c. walnuts, coarsely chopped

Preheat oven to 325°. Oil 3 8" cake pans. Set out ½ c. butter, & 1 8 oz. pkg. cream cheese to soften (for frosting). Put pineapple in sieve to drain. Beat eggs in large bowl. Add sugars and beat till light & fluffy. Add oil & mix well with whisk. Put in the dry ingredients & beat till smooth. Stir in remaining ingredients & pour batter into oiled layer pans. Bake for 40 minutes or until knife comes out clean when inserted in center of cake. Cool slightly and frost.

Frosting

½ c. butter
8 oz. cream cheese
1 1 lb. box powdered sugar
3 tsp. vanilla

Mix together till smooth. Frost between layers & on top. Try toasted coconut for decoration. ♥

COCONUT
LAYER ◯ CAKE
WITH LEMON FILLING

T his is an old-fashioned, big tall coconut cake, the perfect summer cake, three soft layers with a heavenly lemon filling, frosted with a wonderful marshmallow-like frosting & covered in coconut.

Lemon Filling

juice & grated rind of 2 lemons
1 c. sugar
2 eggs, beaten
2 Tbsp. butter, melted

hen grating rind take special care not to get the bitter white part. Put all ingred. in double boiler, stir over simmering water till thickened ~15-20 min. Chill.

Cake

Makes 3 8" layers

6 Tbsp. butter, room temp.
1½ c. sugar
3 eggs, separated
2¼ c. flour, sifted

3 tsp. baking powder
¼ tsp. salt
3/4 c. milk
1 tsp. vanilla

P reheat oven to 350°. Cream butter & sugar. Add egg yolks & beat until thick & lemon-colored. With a fork, mix together dry ingred. & add them to egg mixture alternately with the milk; stir in vanilla. Fold in stiffly beaten egg whites. Divide batter between 3 buttered 8" cake pans. Bake at 350° for 20 min. Cool completely & remove from pans. Before frosting cut off rough edges of cake with sharp scissors.

perfect birthday cake

Continued →

WONDERFUL
MARSHMALLOW-LIKE
Frosting

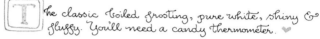

The classic boiled frosting, pure white, shiny & fluffy. You'll need a candy thermometer. ♥

⅓ c. water	pinch of salt
1 c. sugar	2 egg whites
⅛ tsp. cream of tartar	1 tsp. vanilla
sweetened coconut	

Stir the water, sugar, cream of tartar & salt together in a small heavy-bottomed pan. Hook a candy thermometer to the edge of the pan & boil without stirring until mixture reaches 240° F. Meanwhile, beat egg whites until stiff. Pour the 240° syrup over the whites in a thin stream, beating constantly until thick & glossy. Stir in vanilla. Frost the cake ~ pat & sprinkle coconut onto sides & over the top. ♥

To Assemble

Put the chilled filling between cooled layers ~ try not to let too much of it get out the sides. Frost the cake then sprinkle on coconut thickly, gently pressing it into the sides. During this process the cake may try to slip & slide, but just slide it back straight. I decorate the cake with 3 raspberries in the center with 3 lemon balm leaves ❧ , or with a tiny cluster of currant berries, or around the ❧ outside edge with blueberries; especially charming sprinkled with violets. ♥

"Women sit or move to and fro, some
old, some young. The young are
beautiful ~ but the old are more
beautiful than the young."
Walt Whitman ♥

LEMON ROLL

375° Serves Ten

A luscious, really beautiful cake — it's so soft & delicate it reminds me of a newborn baby — you'll see what I mean. It's easy & it's elegant. ♥

3 eggs, separated	1 tsp. baking powder
1 c. sugar	1/4 tsp. salt
6 Tbsp. hot water	grated rind of 1 lemon
1 c. flour	Lemon Filling

powdered sugar

Preheat oven to 375°. Beat egg yolks, add sugar & beat till thick & lemon-colored. Stir in water & dry ingredients. Fold in stiffly beaten egg whites. Add grated rind. Grease a cookie sheet that has a rim (jelly roll pan), line it with waxed paper & grease it again. Pour batter into pan, spreading evenly. Bake 12~15 min. Immediately cut off crisp edges & turn out onto large cloth covered LIGHTLY with powdered sugar. Remove waxed paper. Using the cloth, roll up the cake ▭ & set aside while you make the filling. When ready, unroll cake, spread on filling & roll back up. Cool completely; transfer to serving dish. Cut with serrated knife ♥.

Lemon Filling

1 c. sugar	Put all ingredients in double
2 eggs	boiler — beat well & stir till
2 Tbsp. butter, melted	thick — 15-20 min. Cool slightly.
juice & grated rind of 2 lemons	♥

HEART-SHAPED
STRAWBERRY SHORTCAKE

A delicious way to say I love you. ♥ Cream biscuits make the perfect delicate base for fresh berries. You'll need a heart-shaped cookie cutter, about 2 inches. ♥

*T*o prepare strawberries & make them juicy: Keep back a few small, whole berries for garnish. Cut the rest in bite-sized pieces; sprinkle a couple of spoonfuls of sugar over & toss gently. Refrigerate for 1 hour.

BISCUITS

2 c. unbleached flour
1 tbsp. baking powder
1 tsp. salt

2½ tsp. sugar
1½ c. heavy cream
4 tbsp. melted butter

*P*reheat oven to 425°. With a fork, stir together flour, baking powder, salt & sugar. Slowly add 1 to 1½ c. cream, stirring constantly, just until dough comes together. Place dough on floured board & knead for 1 minute. Pat dough flat to about ¾" thick. Cut with heart-shaped or round 2" cookie cutter & brush both sides with melted butter. Place them 1" apart on ungreased cookie sheet. Bake 15-18 min. till browned. (Makes about 14.)

To Serve *W*hip cream with a spoon of sugar & a tsp. of vanilla, to taste. Split biscuits, spoon berries over bottom half — add a dollop of whipped cream, replace top ~ more berries & cream.

Chocolate Cake

350° Serves 8-12

Rich, dense & fudge-like. Use the very best chocolate you can find♥

11 oz. semi-sweet chocolate	6 lg. eggs, separated
2/3 c. butter	2/3 c. sugar

unsweetened cocoa or flour for dusting pan

Preheat oven to 350°. Butter a 9" springform pan, line the bottom with buttered wax paper; dust pan with cocoa or flour & shake out extra. Slowly melt chocolate & butter together in a heavy saucepan over low heat; cool. Meanwhile separate eggs into 2 large bowls. Beat yolks for about 1 min; slowly add sugar & continue beating till thick & lemon-colored. Beat whites until they just begin to peak. Add cooled chocolate mixture to egg yolks & blend thoroughly. Pour the chocolate & yolk mixture into egg whites & fold gently until completely blended. Pour batter into prepared pan & bake 40-45 min. Cool 1/2 hr. before turning out onto serving plate. Frost with

Chocolate Glaze

1/2 c. whipping cream	4 oz. unsweetened chocolate
3 Tbsp. unsalted butter	4 oz. milk chocolate

Chop chocolates. Simmer cream & butter. Reduce heat; add both chocolates & stir until smooth. Let stand until cool, but still pourable, about 1 hr. Spoon glaze over cake. Refrigerate cake, but serve at room temp. Serve with a spoonful of sweetened whipped cream.

To Decorate To make this luscious cake even More beautiful, cut a piece of wax paper that covers the top of cake. In the center draw the outline of a leaf (use a real leaf). Cut it out - lay the paper over cold cake & shake over a little powdered sugar. Carefully remove wax paper & voilà! You can do this with hearts too, or holly. ♥

ICE CREAM CAKE ROLL

350° Serves Eight

Tender, rich chocolate cake, filled with creamy vanilla ice cream & draped in hot fudge sauce — too good. ♥

¼ c. cocoa

1¼ c. powdered sugar

5 eggs

1 tsp. vanilla

¼ tsp. salt

1 qt. good vanilla ice cream

Preheat oven to 350°. Sift cocoa & sugar together. Separate the eggs; put the yolks & vanilla in a large bowl & beat very well until thick. In another bowl whisk the egg whites till foamy; add salt & continue beating till soft peaks are formed. Fold the cocoa & sugar into the whites, then gently fold ⅓ of egg white mixture into the beaten yolks. Thoroughly butter a 10" × 15" cookie sheet & line it with wax paper. Spread the batter evenly in the pan; bake 18~20 min., until knife comes out clean. Sprinkle a clean tea towel with powdered sugar & turn cake out onto it. Remove wax paper & trim off any crispy edges. Roll the cake in the towel from the long end ⬆ & let it rest 1~2 min. Unroll & let it rest again for a few min., then roll it up again & allow it to cool completely. Set ice cream out to soften. Unroll the cooled cake; spread evenly with ice cream & roll it back up (without the tea towel). Dust the top with powdered sugar. Keep it in the freezer till ready to serve. When ready, cut the cake & serve it with the hot chocolate sauce on the side. ♥

Hot Fudge Sauce

3 Tbsp. unsalted butter

4 oz. unsweetened chocolate

⅔ c. boiling water

1½ c. sugar

7 Tbsp. corn syrup

1 tsp. vanilla

Melt the butter & chocolate in a heavy saucepan over low heat; add boiling water & stir well. Mix in the sugar & corn syrup~till sauce is smooth. Boil the sauce, without stirring, for 10 min.; remove from heat; cool 20 min., then add the vanilla. Spoon the sauce over the ice cream cake and serve. ♥

Boston Cream Pie

Makes 8 glorious servings

Well, this is my first "two-pager" & I promise you, it's well worth it! I love traditional foods & this is Boston Cream Pie at its most outrageous: creamy & chocolaty, with a light cake — 3 heavenly textures in one. ♥

Cream Filling

2 egg yolks
1½ Tbsp. flour
1 Tbsp. cornstarch
¼ c. powdered sugar

1½ c. whole milk
1 Tbsp. butter
½ c. whipping cream
1 tsp. vanilla

Beat the yolks in a double boiler; stir in flour, cornstarch, sugar, milk & butter. Cook over boiling water about 20 min. till thick, stirring constantly. Chill mixture. When cold, whip the cream with the vanilla & fold together. Refrigerate. ♥

Sponge Cake

3 eggs, separated
¼ c. cold water
3/4 c. sugar
½ tsp. vanilla
¼ tsp. lemon zest

3/4 c. cake flour
¼ tsp. baking powder
⅛ tsp. salt
½ tsp. cream of tartar

Preheat oven to 325°. Separate eggs — yolks into lg. bowl, whites into smaller ♥. Beat the yolks for 5 min.;

Continued...

gradually add cold water & beat 1 minute. Add sugar gradually & beat 3 more minutes. Stir in vanilla & lemon zest. In another bowl, mix together flour, baking powder & salt with a fork. Add to yolk mixture in thirds, folding in. Beat the whites with the cream of tartar till they form soft peaks. Fold into yolk mixture. Turn into 2 ungreased 8" cake pans. Bake at 325° for 15~20 min. till golden & springs back to touch. Cool upside down. Run a sharp knife around outside & remove cakes from pan. Refrigerate. When ready to frost (when cream & cake are chilled) make the

Chocolate Icing

2 squares unsweetened chocolate (2 oz)   1 egg yolk
3/4 c. powdered sugar   3 Tbsp. cream
1 Tbsp. water   1/2 tsp. vanilla

Melt chocolate in top of double boiler, remove from heat. Beat in sugar & water at once. Add yolk, beat well. Beat in cream, 1 Tbsp. at a time, then vanilla ♥.

♪ Ta~Daa ♪...

Put the cream filling between cake layers. Spread the chocolate over the top, allowing some to dribble over edges. Keep cake refrigerated. ♥

NOTHIN' SAYS LOVIN' LIKE SOMETHIN' FROM THE OVEN

COOKIES

THERE'S NOTHIN' TO IT, YOU JUST DO IT.

One blustery Fall day my neighbor called me to the white picket fence that runs between my kitchen garden & her kitchen door. I had taken to her the first time we met — she was Harriet Nelson, Aunt Bea, Betty Crocker & my Girl Scout leader Mrs. Hutton all rolled into one — at 70 she was still beautiful. In her hands was a freshly baked, still-warm Sweet Potato Pie covered with a very old, well-worn linen cloth with a thin green stripe down the side & a tiny frayed hole in the corner. She had, for NO REASON, baked us a pie!

Peggy was her name & nurture was her game. She was the beloved oldest sister of 5 girls & she had raised 7 sons of her own. She has gone to heaven now & it's not the same around here without her.

How to Bake a Peggy Pie...

Fill a Whole Lifetime with Equal parts of
Kindness, Humility, Service & Love.
Add a Sympathetic Heart &
A Gentle Spirit.
Spread over All God's Blessings of
Contentedness, Faith & Family.
Serve with Charm & Grace.

AND DON'T FORGET TO SHARE SOME WITH YOUR NEIGHBOR.

SWEET POTATO PIE

475° Serves Eight

This pie has a crunchy pecan topping & a smooth, spicy middle — good hot or cold; try it for Thanksgiving 🦃.

1 9 in. homemade pie shell	3 beaten eggs
½ c. chopped pecans	1 tsp. vanilla
2 c. cooked sweet potatoes	⅓ c. sugar
6 Tbsp. softened butter	1 tsp. cinnamon
¼ c. heavy cream	½ tsp. nutmeg

Preheat oven to 475°. Make your favorite pie shell — prick all over with fork & spread pecans in bottom. Bake 5 min. Cool. Lower heat to 300°. Mash together potatoes & butter till smooth. Add all other ingredients & blend well. Pour into pie shell. Make the

Topping

3 Tbsp. melted butter	½ c. brown sugar
⅔ c. pecans, finely chopped	⅓ c. flour

Combine all ingredients till crumbly. Sprinkle over top of pie. Put the pie on a cookie sheet & bake at 300° for 25~30 min. till golden brown. Delicious with whipped cream or ice cream. ♥

BLUEBERRY
PIE

425°

I feel so lucky because the first summer after I bought my little house on the Vineyard I discovered that it was surrounded by wild blueberry bushes. ♥ And this recipe is the delicious result. I also freeze them so we can have pies in the winter ~ so if you don't have them fresh in your area, frozen ones are fine. ♥

Pie crust dough for two-crust 8" pie (p. 27)
4 c. blueberries (if frozen, its not necessary to defrost)
3/4 c. sugar
3½ Tbsp. flour
pinch of salt
squeeze of fresh lemon juice
1 Tbsp. butter

Preheat oven to 425°. Make the pie crust and use half to line an 8" pie plate. In a large bowl mix sugar, flour, and salt. Add blueberries and a squeeze of lemon and mix well. Pour mixture into pie pan & dot evenly with butter. Cover with top crust, trim edges, fold them under & crimp edges. Cut vents in top. Bake for 10 min; lower heat to 325°. Bake 40 min. till top is brown. Serve with vanilla ice cream. ♥

BANANA CREAM PIE

This pie is luscious!   Serves Eight

½ c. sugar
6 Tbsp. flour
¼ tsp. salt
2½ c. milk
2 egg yolks
1 Tbsp. butter

½ tsp. vanilla extract
3 ripe bananas
1 baked 9" pie shell (p.27)
½ c. shredded coconut
1½ c. cream, whipped

Mix sugar, flour & salt in the top part of a double boiler. Gradually stir in milk and cook over boiling water ~ stir constantly until thickened. Cover & cook 10 min. longer, stirring occasionally. Beat egg yolks & add to them a small amount of milk mixture. Return mixture to the double boiler & cook for 2 min. over hot, not boiling, water. Stir constantly. Remove from heat ~ stir in butter & extract. Cool. Slice 2 bananas into bottom of pie shell and arrange evenly. Pour cooked mixture over bananas and refrigerate. Spread coconut on a cookie sheet and toast at 350° ~ it burns easily so stir often. Before serving, cover pie with whipped cream, arrange remaining sliced banana around the edge of pie, and put the toasted coconut in the center.

CHEESECAKE

My dear friend Laney gave me this recipe about 15 years ago and I still haven't tried one that's better ~ It's a perfect cheesecake and requires no frills.

crust

2½ c. graham cracker crumbs
3/4 c. melted butter

Combine and press into a buttered 9 in. pie plate, building up sides.

filling

1 8 oz. pkg. cream cheese, softened
½ c. sugar
1 Tbsp. lemon juice
½ tsp. vanilla extract
dash salt
2 eggs

Beat softened cream cheese till fluffy. Gradually blend in sugar, lemon juice, vanilla, and salt. Add eggs, one at a time; beat after each. Pour filling into crust. Bake at 325° for 25~30 min., till set.

topping

1½ c. sour cream
3 Tbsp. sugar
3/4 tsp. vanilla

Combine all ingredients and spoon over top of hot cheese~ cake. Bake 10 min. longer. Cool ~ Chill several hours.

CHOCOLATE MOUSSE PIE

Serves Ten

A chocolate dream in a chocolate cookie crust. ♥

Crust:

1½ pkgs. chocolate wafer cookies, crushed
1 Tbsp. fresh coffee granules
6 Tbsp. butter, melted (or more)

Combine all ingredients ~ use additional butter if you think it needs it ~ you'll want it to hold together when you cut it. Reserve about 2 Tbsp. for garnish. Press into 9" pie plate.

Mousse:

1 Tbsp. unflavored gelatin	8 oz. semisweet chocolate
⅓ c. rum	1 Tbsp. instant coffee powder
½ c. sugar	¼ c. butter, cut into teaspoonfuls
5 eggs, separated	2 c. heavy cream, whipped
¾ c. crème de cacao	1 c. heavy cream, whipped (garnish)

Combine gelatin & rum in a small bowl. Mix well & set aside. Separate eggs ~ reserve whites. Combine sugar & egg yolks in top part of double boiler; beat 3 min. till thickened. Stir in crème de cacao & set over simmering water, beating constantly till mixture is hot & foamy. Remove from heat; add gelatin mixture; beat for 5-6 min. till mixture is cool; set aside. Melt chocolate very slowly in a heavy saucepan. Stir in instant coffee; remove from heat & beat in butter, 1 tsp. at a time. Very slowly, stir the chocolate into egg mixture; beat until mixture is room temperature. Beat reserved egg whites until stiff; fold them into the whipped cream & then fold all into chocolate mixture. Pour into prepared pie plate & refrigerate at least 4 hours. Garnish with additional whipped cream & reserved cookie crumbs. ♥

OLD-FASHIONED
APPLE PIE

450° Serves Eight

This is the kind of country pie they used to make in the "good old days"—with a tall top crust filled with juicy apples.

14 green apples, peeled, cored & sliced   ¼ tsp. salt
1 c. brown sugar   3½ Tbsp. cornstarch
1 tsp. cinnamon   1 Tbsp. lemon juice
½ tsp. nutmeg   2 Tbsp. butter

Combine all ingredients except butter. Pour into pie shell, piling high in the middle. Dot with butter. Cover with top crust. Cut out vents in top center. Bake on cookie sheet 10 min. at 450°, reduce heat to 350° & bake 40~50 min. longer till apples are tender & crust is brown. ♥

Pie Crust

4 c. unbleached flour.   2 c. Crisco shortening
2 tsp. salt   ice water to form ball

♥ Chill all ingredients—1 hr.

Put the flour & salt in a bowl & cut in Crisco with pastry cutter to the size of small peas. Slowly add ice water, stirring with fork till dough comfortably holds together in a ball. Flour a board & rolling pin. You'll need a bottom crust ⅛" thick & about 10" in diameter & a top crust of at least 16" in diameter. Divide dough accordingly & roll out bottom crust; put into 8" pie dish. Fill with apples; lay over top crust, fold & crimp edges. See above to finish. ♥

SWEET DREAMS

SWEET STUFF

SWEET TOOTH

Sweet Nothing

SPREAD A SLICE OF SOFT
WHITE BREAD WITH
SOFTENED BUTTER
& SPRINKLE
WITH SUGAR.
BEST EATEN IN COOL
SUNSHINE.

(on rollerskates)

SWEETHEARTS

(COO)

SWEETIE PIE

SWEET
PEA

Sugar is Sweet and so are You ♥

FRUIT

DESSERTS

CHOCOLATE POACHED PEARS

Serves 6

1 c. sugar
2 c. water
1 c. white sherry
½ Vanilla bean, split lengthwise
juice of one lemon

6 ripe Bosc pears, peeled, cored,
    leaving stem intact
1½ pts. vanilla ice cream,
    softened
Chocolate Sauce (below)

In a 4 qt. non-aluminum pan, combine sugar, water, sherry, vanilla bean & lemon juice; bring to simmer over med. low heat. Peel, & core the pears from the bottom; leave stems on. Arrange the pears in the simmering syrup so that they are not pressed too tightly together. Cover & poach 15~25 min., until tender, but still fairly firm when pierced. Chill pears in liquid, basting occasionally. Just before serving, make Chocolate Sauce.

Chocolate Sauce

1½ Tbsp. unsalted butter
2 oz. unsweetened chocolate
⅓ c. boiling water

3/4 c. sugar
3½ Tbsp. corn syrup
½ tsp. vanilla extract

Melt butter & chocolate in a heavy saucepan over low heat; add boiling water & stir well. Stir in sugar & corn syrup till smooth. Boil 10 min. without stirring. Remove from heat; allow to cool 10 min. Stir in vanilla. While chocolate is cooling, let ice cream soften. Scoop ice cream onto dessert dish ~ set a pear on top & drizzle over warm chocolate sauce ... m-m-m-m ... serve. ♥

BANANA FRITTERS

4-5 Servings

This is a very special dessert, crunchy on the outside, soft in the middle ⟶.

1 egg	2 tsp. melted butter
⅓ c. milk	4 bananas
½ c. flour	juice of one lemon
2 tsp. sugar	2 Tbsp. powdered sugar
½ tsp. baking powder	cooking oil
½ tsp. salt	sour cream (or ice cream)

Separate the egg & beat the white until stiff. Beat the yolk with milk. Stir in the flour mixed with sugar, baking powder, and salt. Stir in the melted butter. Fold in beaten egg white. Cut the bananas into chunks and squeeze the lemon juice over them. Sprinkle them with the powdered sugar. Dip the banana pieces into the batter and fry in two inches of hot oil. Top with sour cream or ice cream, and serve immediately ♥

BANANA ICE CREAM

Easy, and healthy. Take frozen banana chunks from your freezer, put in blender with milk to cover, add a tsp. of coffee and a tsp. of vanilla. Blend, serve, yum. ♥ ♥ ♥ ♥

PEACH & PLUM CRISP

350° Serves 8-10

Thank goodness for good friends, otherwise who could feel comfortable serving a pie with a piece already missing? I only meant to taste the edge of topping & then the phone rang & I picked, nibbled, got a spoon & _did_ the pie. I should call it "Bye Pie." WAVE BYE-BYE.

Filling:
4 med. peaches, peeled & pitted
2½ lbs. plums, pitted
½ c. sugar
2 Tbsp. quick-cooking tapioca
1 tsp. fresh lemon juice
pinch of salt

Topping:
½ c. butter, softened
½ c. brown sugar
¾ c. flour
¾ c. oats
¼ c. chopped walnuts
2 tsp. lemon zest
½ tsp. cinnamon

Butter a 10 in. glass or pottery pie plate (2" deep). Peel peaches by dipping each briefly in boiling water. Cut them & plums into wedges. Mix together all ingred. for filling, put into pie plate. Let stand 1 hr.; stir occasionally. Preheat oven to 350°. Mix together topping ingred., spread evenly over fruit. Bake on center rack in oven; put a cookie sheet on lower rack to catch juices. Serve hot with ice cream or cold with whipped cream. ♥ (Good with phone too. ♥)

"Charm: the quality in others that makes us more satisfied with ourselves."

♥ Henri-Frédérik Amiel

Chocolate-Dipped Strawberries.

Sweets to the sweet — romance in berry form.

Melt really good bittersweet chocolate in a small heavy pan. Dip large (washed & dried) perfectly ripe strawberries into the chocolate — put them on waxed paper to set. Keep refrigerated. Serve with a glass of pink champagne. ☺

"To Know, Know, Know You is to Love, Love, Love You."

Phil Spector

BAKED APPLE

350° Serves one

An old~fashioned, homey thing to have for break~
fast — it makes your kitchen smell like heaven. ♥

1 Tbsp. oats   pinch of cinnamon
½ Tbsp. brown sugar   pinch of nutmeg
½ Tbsp. chopped walnuts   dash of lemon juice
2 tsp. soft butter   1 Tbsp. apple juice
1 apple, Cortland or Rome Beauty ~ good for baking

Preheat oven to 350°. Wash & core the apple, being
careful not to break through bottom ~ do a nice
wide core so there's lots of room for the filling.
Mix together all the rest of the ingredients except
for apple juice. Fill the apple with the mixture &
put it in a shallow baking dish. Pour the apple
juice around the apple & bake for 25 min, till
tender. Serve warm with heavy cream poured
over. ♥

"Nothing happens to any man that he
is not formed by nature to bear."
Marcus Aurelius

CHERRIES JUBILEE

Serves 6

Hot, brandied cherries poured over vanilla ice cream—wonderful because you can keep the ingredients on hand & be ready for a surprise dessert. ❤

¼ c. sugar
dash salt
1½ Tbsp. cornstarch
2 cans (16½ oz. each) pitted dark
  sweet cherries in syrup
4 Tbsp. brandy
1½ pts. good vanilla ice cream

In a large skillet mix together sugar, salt & cornstarch; add syrup from cherries, but reserve cherries for later. Bring to a boil, stirring constantly until thickened. Reduce heat to simmer & gently stir in cherries. Warm the brandy, ignite it & pour over cherries. Scoop ice cream into dessert dishes & pour hot cherries over. ❤

"The days are short, the weather's cold, by tavern fires tales are told."

New England Almanac, Dec. 1704

APPLE CRISP

375° Serves Six

An old standby with a deliciously crunchy top. Serve it either hot or cold — pour thick cream over or serve with ice cream.

About 4 medium, peeled, sliced, tart apples (Granny Smith)
3/4 c. firmly packed brown sugar
1/2 c. flour
1/2 c. oats
3/4 tsp. cinnamon
3/4 tsp. nutmeg
1/3 c. softened butter

Preheat oven. Butter a square baking pan. Place the apple slices in pan. Mix remaining ingredients and sprinkle over apples. Bake 30 minutes or until apples are tender and topping is golden brown.

" My garden will never make me famous,
I'm a horticultural ignoramus,
I can't tell a stringbean from a soybean,
Or even a girl bean from a boy bean."
Ogden Nash

Strawberry Cheesecake
♥ chocolate crust ♥

Follow recipe on a box of Oreo Chocolate Cookie Crumbs for a 9" pie crust. ♥

♥ filling ♥

1 8 oz. pkg. cream cheese, softened
1/2 c. sugar
1 tbsp. lemon juice

1/2 tsp. vanilla
dash salt
2 eggs

Beat softened cream cheese till fluffy. Gradually blend in sugar, lemon juice, vanilla & salt. Add eggs, one at a time; beat well after each. Pour filling into crust. Bake at 325° for 25-30 min., till set.

♥ topping ♥

1 1/2 c. sour cream
3 tbsp. sugar
3/4 tsp. vanilla

Combine all ingredients & spoon over top of hot pie. Bake 10 min. more. Cool ~ chill well.

♥ strawberry glaze ♥

Cover top of pie with washed & stemmed, perfect, fresh strawberries, pointed end up. Slowly bring 1/2 c. clear red currant jelly or strawberry jelly (clear, no seeds) & 1 tsp. lemon juice to a slow boil, stirring. Spoon or brush glaze over berries — refrigerate. ♥

"You must always be awaggle with love."
D.H. Lawrence

APPLE FRITTERS

Serves 6

Every child's gourmet dream come true! But definitely not for children only. Great at breakfast, delicious for tea, but best of all as a surprise treat — like after playing in the snow, or after school to celebrate the start of Christmas vacation. ♥

4 lg. sweet apples,
  McIntosh or
  Cortland
6 c. vegetable oil
1½ c. unbleached flour
⅛ tsp. salt

12 oz. beer, at room
  temperature
extra flour
½ c. sugar
¾ tsp. cinnamon

Peel, core & slice apples into ½" rings ◎. In a deep pot, heat oil to 350°. Mix together 1½ c. flour, salt & beer; beat well. Put about a cup more of flour into another small bowl. Mix sugar with cinnamon & set aside. Coat apple rings in flour, cover completely with beer batter. Fry in hot oil, a few at a time, for about 4 min. till golden. Drain on paper towels, roll in cinnamon sugar & serve. They can be very hot inside, so be careful! ♥

I heard this on T.V. and thought you'd like a little chuckle while you make these fritters — here goes: "Did you hear they're opening a restaurant on the moon? Great food, but no atmosphere!" Ha Ha Ha ⌣

GREEN APPLE
& BLUEBERRY TART

400° Serves 6~8

This is a rustic country pie ~ it's free-form & easy to make.

½ lb. frozen puff pastry, thawed
  (available at grocery stores)
4 green apples, peeled, cored,
  cut into ¼" slices
1 c. fresh (or frozen) blueberries
2 Tbsp. fresh lemon juice

¼ c. brown sugar
2 Tbsp. white sugar
2 Tbsp. flour
¾ tsp. cinnamon
1 Tbsp. butter
powdered sugar

Preheat oven to 400°. Roll out pastry to a 14"
circle on a lightly floured surface. Transfer
to a large cookie sheet & chill. Put fruit
in a large bowl & toss with lemon juice.
Add sugars, flour & cinnamon, mix well. Evenly
arrange fruit mixture in center of pastry, leaving
a 2" border. Fold edge of pastry up & over apple mixture
in overlapping folds to form sides of pie. (There should be a
4 to 5" opening in the middle — feel comfortable, nothing here
is supposed to be perfect.) Brush folds with a little water
at edges & pinch to seal. Cut butter into bits over fruit;
sprinkle tart with a little granulated sugar & bake 40
min. If pastry gets too brown, cover tart with a piece of
foil. Cool 10 min., slide onto serving plate. Sift over a bit
of powdered sugar & serve. ♡

"One comes back to these old-fashioned roses as
one does to music and old poetry. A
garden needs old associations, old fragrances, as
a home needs things that have been lived
with."
♡ Marion Page

39

FRUIT DESSERTS

Sliced Peaches & Cream
Briefly dip whole ripe peaches into boiling water, peel with a sharp knife & cut into slices. Sprinkle with sugar & chill at least one hour. Serve with or without a wee soupçon of heavy cream.

Cantaloupe & Ice Cream
Cut a cantaloupe in half, scrape out seeds & fill cavity with a scoop of vanilla ice cream. Great for a special brunch.

Lemon Ice
Hollow out **whole lemons** & fill them with Lemon Ice & freeze them. To serve: pile them in a pyramid & tuck in mint sprigs. Recipe: 3½ c. water 1¼ c. sugar ¾ c. fresh lemon juice 2 Tbsp. lemon zest. Boil water, stir in sugar until dissolved, add lemon juice & zest & freeze in a bowl. Remove from freezer, beat till fluffy, fill lemons & refreeze till ready to serve.

Watermelon Surprise
Remove visible seeds from a slice of watermelon, spread with sour cream & sprinkle over brown sugar. (The surprise happens when your tastebuds explode!)

Chocolate~Dipped Strawberries
Dip whole perfect ripe strawberries into melted bittersweet chocolate. Set on waxed paper to dry.

Red, White & Blueberry Sundaes
Strawberry ice cream drizzled with blueberry sauce topped with whipped cream & a big fresh strawberry. Blueberry Sauce ⟶ next page

Blueberry Sauce
Delicious over ice cream.

12 oz. fresh or frozen wild blueberries, 1/3 c. water, 1/3 c. sugar, & 1 tsp. grated lemon rind. Place all ingredients in a non-aluminum saucepan & bring to a boil. Simmer gently for 10 min. Serve hot or cold. ♥

Fruit Fondue with Orange Chocolate Sauce

Skewer fresh strawberries, pineapple, bananas, pears, apples & pieces of angel food cake & dip them into this heated chocolate sauce: 12 oz. semi-sweet chocolate, 2/3 c. heavy cream & 2 tbsp. orange liqueur. Heat chocolate & cream, stirring over low heat 'till chocolate melts. Stir in liqueur. Keep warm over very low heat. ♥

Watermelon Whale
Cut a whole watermelon into the shape of a whale & hollow it out.
Fill   VIEW FROM THE TOP   the cavity with
fresh   fruit, strawberries, cantaloupe (use a melon baller), raspberries, red grapes, bananas, & watermelon.   Darling at a pot luck barbecue or picnic. ♥

Baked Bananas with Ice Cream
Put one ripe banana per person on a cookie sheet (in its skin). Bake at 350° until it turns completely black, about 20 min. Slit open & moosh up, same as you would with a baked potato. Serve with a scoop of vanilla ice cream & a sprinkle of fresh ground coffee. ♥

Almost Fruit ~ for the kids
Hollow out halved oranges & fill with Jell-O. Serve with a dot of whipped cream. This makes 10 halves: make a 6 oz. pkg. of Jell-O according to instructions except use only 1½ c. boiling water. ♥

CHERRY ORANGES!

DESSERT!   DESSERT!   DESSERT!

41

3 Fruit Sauces

DELICIOUS ON WAFFLES, PANCAKES, FRENCH TOAST, GERMAN PANCAKE, & ICE CREAM

MAKES 2 CUPS
   20 OZ. BAG FROZEN, WHOLE STRAWBERRIES
   1/2 C. WATER
   1/2 C. SUGAR
COARSELY CHOP 2/3 OF THE BERRIES – SET ASIDE
THE REST. PUT CHOPPED BERRIES, WATER, AND SUGAR
IN A STAINLESS S. SAUCEPAN AND BRING TO A BOIL.
REDUCE HEAT TO MEDIUM AND CONTINUE TO COOK
15 MIN. STIR IN WHOLE BERRIES AND HEAT
THROUGH. SERVE WARM.

MAKES 2 CUPS
   3 LG. GREEN APPLES (GRANNY SMITH)
   1 C. WATER
   1 TBSP. SUGAR
   1 TSP. CINNAMON
PEEL, CORE, AND COARSELY CHOP APPLES. PUT ALL
INGREDIENTS IN A STAINLESS S. SAUCEPAN AND BRING
TO A BOIL. REDUCE HEAT TO MEDIUM AND CONTINUE TO
COOK 10 MINUTES, STIRRING OFTEN. SERVE WARM.

MAKES 1 1/3 CUPS
   12 OZ. BAG FROZEN BLUEBERRIES
   1/3 C. WATER
   1/3 C. SUGAR
   1 TSP. GRATED LEMON RIND
PLACE ALL INGREDIENTS IN A STAINLESS S. SAUCEPAN AND BRING TO A BOIL.
REDUCE HEAT TO MEDIUM – COOK 5 MIN. GENTLY STRAIN OUT BERRIES AND CON-
TINUE COOKING LIQUID 5 MORE MIN. (THIS HELPS TO KEEP BERRIES INTACT.)
RETURN BERRIES TO JUICE AND HEAT THROUGH. SERVE WARM.

RASPBERRY
SAUCE

Makes 1 cup

Spoon some of this beautiful red sauce onto a
plate & set a scoop of Orange Ice (p.59) on top.
Or try it with a slice of Chocolate Cake (p.16).
Also good with ice cream and/or waffles. ♥

2 c. fresh (or frozen) raspberries
2 Tbsp. currant jelly
1–2 Tbsp. sugar
1 tsp. cornstarch

Crush the raspberries & force through sieve to
remove seeds. Put the raspberry juice, along with
the jelly, into a small saucepan & bring to a boil.
Add sugar to taste; simmer 2 min. Mix the
cornstarch with 1 Tbsp. cold water till smooth;
slowly whisk mixture into sauce. Cook, stirring,
5–7 min. till thickened. Chill. ♥

L-O-DOUBLE-L-I- P-O-P
SPELLS LOLLIPOP (LOLLIPOP ♪)
THAT'S THE ONLY DECENT
KIND OF CANDY (CANDY)
THE MAN WHO
MADE IT SURELY WAS A
DANDY (DANDY)
L-O-DOUBLE-L-I-
P-O-P-U-C IT'S A
LICK ON A STICK
GUARANTEED TO
MAKE YOU SICK
BUT IT'S LOLLIPOP
FOR ME- E-E. ♪

Puddings

Candy

Ices

Confections

Ice Cream Concoctions

& much much

More

TOO MUCH OF A GOOD THING CAN BE WONDERFUL

RICE PUDDING

My mother's favorite dessert. I like to serve it with whipped cream or just plain cream poured over the top. I think it's a comforting type of dessert, good in the wintertime, and not unhealthful. ♥

2 c cooked brown rice
3 c whole milk (or whatever you like)
¼ c brown sugar
1 c raisins
½ tsp. mixed cinnamon & nutmeg
3 eggs, beaten

Beat the eggs in a large bowl. Add all the other ingredients and mix well. Pour into oiled casserole. Bake at 325° for about one hour, or until set. Serve it hot or cold. The pudding looks good in an old fashioned dish or heavy pottery. ♥

ONE PINT
MILK

TAPIOCA PUDDING

Serves Eight

Light & delicate—there is something comforting & old-fashioned about this dessert. ♥

4 eggs, separated
3 3/4 c. whole milk
6 Tbsp. quick tapioca
10 Tbsp. sugar
1/4 tsp. salt
2 tsp. vanilla
zest of 1 lemon

Slightly beat egg yolks in heavy saucepan; stir in milk, tapioca, 6 Tbsp. sugar, & salt. Let stand 5 min. Bring to full boil over medium heat, stirring constantly; remove from heat. Beat egg whites till frothy, add remaining 4 Tbsp. sugar, & continue beating till stiff. Add whites, vanilla, & grated lemon rind to hot milk mixture & stir to blend. Pour into 8 individual pudding cups & chill. ♥

"Across the gateway of my heart
I wrote 'No Thoroughfare,'
But love came laughing by, and cried:
'I enter everywhere.' "
♥ Herbert Shipman

CHOCOLATE MOUSSE

Serves Eight

8-oz. semisweet chocolate
¼ c. dark rum
½ c. sugar

2-3 Tbsp. lukewarm water
2 egg whites
2 c. heavy cream

Melt chocolate in top of double boiler. Meanwhile cook rum & sugar over very low heat till sugar melts (do not let it brown). Add sugar syrup to chocolate (they should be about the same temp.). Beat in 2 Tbsp. lukewarm water; set aside. Beat egg whites till stiff; whip cream & fold together. Beat chocolate again — if it has thickened, add 1 more Tbsp. water. Fold chocolate into cream & spoon into individual serving dishes or wine glasses. Chill.

CRÈME CARAMEL

325° Serves Eight

Light, delicate and elegant ~ also, totally delicious. This is my
favorite dessert. ♥ When inverted into serving dish the caramel
surrounds the custard like an island. ♥

3 eggs
2 egg yolks
½ c. sugar
2 c. hot milk

1 c. hot cream
1½ tsp. vanilla

♥ ♥ ♥ ♥

¾ c. sugar, melted

Preheat oven to 325° Beat eggs & yolks together, just to blend.
Heat milk and cream together. Stir sugar into eggs; slowly
add hot milk & cream, stirring constantly. Add vanilla. To
make caramel: Put ¾ c. sugar into dry skillet over medium
flame. Swirl pan, but don't stir. Cook till deep caramel color.
It dries as it cools, so work quickly. Divide the caramel
among 8 buttered ramekins & swirl each. Set the dishes
into a roasting pan. Pour boiling water into roasting pan to
about 1" deep. Pour the custard into ramekins, filling about
¾ full. Put the roasting pan into oven for 45 min. till a
knife, inserted in middle, comes out clean. Cool, then chill,
covered in refrigerator. To serve, cut tightly around
ramekin ~ invert small bowl over ramekin ~ turn both upside-
down ~ pudding will slide out. ♥

FATHER'S BREAD PUDDING
With WHISKEY SAUCE

325° Serves 12

1 lg. loaf day-old French bread, cut
   into 3/4" cubes, about 12 c.

3 eggs

2 c. milk

3 Tbsp. vanilla extract

1 c. sugar

3/4 tsp. cinnamon

3/4 tsp. nutmeg

3 c. peeled, sliced tart apples

1 c. cranberries, washed &
       lightly dusted with sugar

Topping

3/4 c. butter, cut into bits

3 Tbsp. cinnamon

2 tsp. nutmeg

Preheat oven to 325°. Butter 9" x 13" baking dish. Put bread into a large colander ~ pour about 4c. hot tap water over bread evenly. Allow to sit 5 min. ~ press out excess water & set aside. In a very lg. bowl, whisk together eggs, milk, vanilla, sugar & spices. Gently fold in bread, apples & cranberries. Pour into prepared dish. Drop butter bits evenly over the top. Mix together cinnamon & nutmeg ~ sprinkle over pudding. Bake 1 hr. & 20 min. Serve warm with hot whiskey sauce. Can be made ahead & baked later. ♥

"Whiskey Sauce

1 c. butter

1 c. sugar

½ c. whiskey

2 eggs, beaten

Melt butter over med. heat. Add sugar, stir constantly till bubbly ~ about 2 min. Remove from heat & slowly stir in whiskey ~ continue cooking & stirring 1 min. Remove from heat & slowly add enough whiskey mixture to eggs to warm them, stirring briskly. Over low heat, stirring, add eggs to whiskey mixture ~ it will thicken. Serve. ♥ Can be gently rewarmed.

Pots de Crème

Serves Four

Smooth, rich chocolate ∼ fast & easy, made in the blender
or food processor ∼ serve in little pots or in glass goblets.♥
We took a trayful of them to a party; everyone loved them!

3/4 c. whole milk
6 oz. semi-sweet chocolate,
   chopped fine
1 lg. egg
2 Tbsp. sugar
1 tsp. vanilla
pinch of salt
3 Tbsp. rum
whipped cream

Heat milk slowly, just to boiling point. Put all other
ingredients except rum & whipped cream into blender or food
processor ∼ slowly add hot milk & blend for 30 seconds. Add
rum & continue blending 1 more minute. Pour into serving
dishes; chill. Serve with a dollop of whipped cream. ♥

INDIAN PUDDING

300° Serves Eight

An old New England favorite, this pudding is best served warm with a big scoop of vanilla ice cream. It's a comforting wintertime dessert. ♥

5½ c. whole milk
⅔ c. cornmeal
4 Tbsp. butter
½ c. maple syrup
¼ c. molasses

1 tsp. ginger
1 tsp. cinnamon
½ tsp. salt
1 c. raisins
vanilla ice cream

Preheat oven to 300°. Butter a small casserole ~ mine is 6½" x 10½". Over med. heat, in a large saucepan, heat the milk but don't boil it. Slowly whisk in cornmeal & continue to stir until mixture begins to thicken ~ 10 min. or so. Add remaining ingredients & keep stirring till heated through. Pour into casserole & bake 3 hours till sides are brown & sticky-looking. (The pudding hardens a bit as it cools.) Serve warm with vanilla ice cream. ♥

"No Spring, nor Summer Beauty
    hath such grace,
As I have seen in one Autumnall face."
    ♥ John Donne

CRÈME de PUMPKIN

325° Serves 6

I can't say enough nice things about this dessert. It is nothing like pumpkin pie, but the most creamy, smooth, delicious pudding-like confection with a snappy crust of caramelized brown sugar on the top. ♥

3 c. heavy cream
6 egg yolks
1 can pumpkin purée (about 2 c.)
½ c. lt. brown sugar
5 tsp. vanilla extract

¼ tsp. ground allspice
1 tsp. ground cloves
¼ tsp. freshly ground nutmeg
¾ c. dark brown sugar (for topping)

(Boil a teapotful of water to use later.) Preheat oven to 325°. Bring cream to boil over medium heat. Meanwhile whisk egg yolks into pumpkin, one at a time. Slowly whisk in lt. brown sugar, then vanilla & spices. When cream has reached boiling point, slowly pour into pumpkin mixture, whisking vigorously. Set an 8" square baking pan into a larger pan & pour the pumpkin mixture into the smaller pan. Place pans into upper half of oven & pour enough boiling water into larger pan to come up half way. Bake 1 hr. to 1 hr. & 10 min. till top is set ~ it will firm as it cools. Remove from water bath ~ made easier by siphoning off the water with a baster. Cover & chill thoroughly. Heat broiler. Sift brown sugar evenly & loosely over the top of pudding ~ set 5"-6" under broiler flame ~ WATCH CLOSELY; rotate often. In only 2-3 min. the sugar will liquefy & caramelize but it will also burn easily (so don't go off to fold the laundry). Serve, or chill first, <u>uncovered</u>. (I love it both ways, but chilled is my favorite.) ♥

PROFITEROLES

375° Makes 12 puffs   Serves 6

¼ c. butter
½ c. water
½ c. flour
2 eggs, room temp.

2 pts. vanilla ice cream, softened
Chocolate Sauce (below)
1 c. heavy cream, whipped with 1 tsp.
   vanilla & sugar to taste

Preheat oven to 375°. Boil butter & water together in a small saucepan. Remove from heat; add flour all at once, beating rapidly till dough leaves side of pan & forms a ball. Cool 5 min. Add eggs, one at a time, beating hard till dough is smooth. Drop teaspoonsful (12) on ungreased cookie sheet 2" apart. Bake 16-20 min. till golden brown. Cool. Set ice cream out to soften. With serrated knife, carefully cut off top 3rd of each puff; remove wet dough inside. Fill with as much ice cream as you can & replace tops. Pile them into a bowl; keep them in freezer till ready to serve (a few hrs.). Make chocolate. When ready, whip cream, reheat chocolate till pourable. Cover frozen puffs with half the chocolate, then the cream. Serve; pass rest of chocolate separately. ♥

Chocolate Sauce: Makes 2 c.: 1 c. sweetened condensed milk; 10 oz. good bittersweet chocolate; ½ c + 1 Tbsp. hot water; ¼ tsp. salt; 2 tsp. vanilla. Combine milk, chocolate, water & salt in heavy pan; stir over low heat till smooth & blended. Stir in vanilla. ♥

LEMON SQUARES

350° *Makes 9 squares*

This recipe helped me get my Girl Scout cooking badge (pictured above: the "credential" that still hangs on my studio wall) — it was the hit of all bake sales! Delicious! 💜

1/2 c. unsalted butter, softened
1 c. unbleached flour

1/4 c. powdered sugar
1/4 tsp. lemon extract
pinch of salt

Preheat oven to 350°. Thoroughly butter an 8" square pan. With an electric mixer, cream all ingredients till soft & smooth. (Or, in a food processor, till it forms a ball.) Press dough evenly into pan & bake 20 min. Meanwhile, make the topping.

2 eggs
1 c. sugar
1/4 tsp. lemon extract
juice & zest of 1 lemon

1/4 c. unbleached flour
1/2 tsp. baking powder
powdered sugar

💜 💜 💜

With electric mixer, beat eggs well & gradually add sugar, until mixture is thick. Gradually add remaining ingredients, except powdered sugar. Continue beating till crust comes out of oven. Pour lemon mixture over hot crust, return it to oven & reduce heat to 325°. Bake 30~35 min. till top is golden. Remove from oven & run a sharp knife around the edge. Cool 20 min.; cut into squares, remove from pan & sift over powdered sugar. 💜 This recipe is easily doubled ~ use juice of 2 lemons but zest from only 1. Second baking time should be increased 3-5 min. 💜

Crunchy Granola Ice Cream Squares with Caramel Sauce

9 Squares

3½ c. really good granola
(say no thankyou to diet granola)
½ c. Hershey's chocolate syrup

1 qt. vanilla ice cream, softened
Caramel Sauce (below)

Spread 2 c. granola evenly in the bottom of a 9"x9" pan. Drizzle chocolate sauce over the granola & spread on the softened ice cream as evenly as possible. Sprinkle remaining 1½ c. granola over ice cream & press down gently & make it level. Freeze till ready to serve. Cut into squares & serve with either cold or heated Caramel Sauce. ♥

Caramel Sauce

1 c. sugar
3 Tbsp. water   1 c. heavy cream

Heat sugar & water together in non~aluminum pan. Bring to simmer & cook without stirring until amber in color. Heat cream in another pan. When sugar is amber, slowly pour in hot cream, whisking constantly until well blended. Good hot or cold. ♥

"KNOW YOU WHAT IT IS TO BE A CHILD? IT IS TO BE VERY DIFFERENT FROM THE MAN OF TODAY. IT IS TO HAVE A SPIRIT YET STREAMING FROM THE WATERS OF BAPTISM; IT IS TO BELIEVE IN LOVE, TO BELIEVE IN LOVELINESS, TO BELIEVE IN BELIEF; IT IS TO BE SO LITTLE THAT THE ELVES CAN REACH TO WHISPER IN YOUR EAR..." ♥ FRANCIS THOMPSON

Snow Clouds

Serves 6-8

This elegant dessert consists of a firm~but~moist meringue, floating cloudlike in a rich, bourbon~flavored custard; all chilled, and served with warm caramel sauce. ♥ yum

Custard

3 C. MILK
1" VANILLA BEAN, SPLIT & SCRAPED
6 LG. EGG YOLKS
1/2 C. SUGAR
1 1/2 TBSP. BOURBON

• • •

Meringue Clouds

3 LG. EGG WHITES
1/2 C. SUGAR

IN A LG. NON-ALUMINUM PAN, HEAT MILK & VANILLA BEAN (WITH SEEDS SCRAPED OUT & INCLUDED)~TO SIMMER. MEANWHILE, IN A SMALL BOWL, BEAT TOGETHER YOLKS, SUGAR & BOURBON. SLOWLY POUR A SMALL AMT. OF HOT MILK INTO YOLK MIXTURE, WHISKING BRISKLY. CONTINUE WHISKING AS YOU SLOWLY POUR YOLKS INTO MILK. OVER LOW HEAT, STIR CONSTANTLY TILL MIXTURE THICKENS TO COAT A SPOON WELL. STRAIN THROUGH A FINE MESH SIEVE INTO A LG. SHALLOW SERVING DISH. SET ASIDE TO COOL WHILE YOU MAKE THE MERINGUE CLOUDS.

♥   ♥   ♥

FILL A LG. SKILLET 2/3 FULL OF WATER & BRING TO A SIMMER ~ DO NOT BOIL.
 BEAT EGG WHITES TILL SOFT PEAKS FORM & SLOWLY ADD 1/2 C. SUGAR ~ BEAT UNTIL STIFF PEAKS FORM. USING 2 WOODEN SPOONS, OR WHATEVER WORKS FOR YOU, FORM WHITES INTO LARGE GOLF BALLS & GENTLY SLIDE THEM INTO THE SIMMER-ING WATER. POACH 4~6 AT A TIME ~ DO NOT LET THEM TOUCH. POACH 7 MIN. ON 1ST SIDE, TURN GENTLY & POACH 3 MORE MIN. DRAIN ON PAPER TOWELS. ARRANGE BALLS ON TOP OF THE COOLED CUSTARD, CLOSE TOGETHER. CHILL.

♥   ♥   ♥

Caramel Sauce

1/4 C. SUGAR
2 TSP. WATER
1/4 C. HEAVY CREAM

IN A SMALL NON-ALUMINUM SAUCEPAN, OVER LOW HEAT, SLOWLY DISSOLVE SUGAR IN WATER. INCREASE HEAT, & CONTINUE TO COOK SUGAR WITHOUT STIRRING UNTIL AMBER IN COLOR. MEANWHILE, IN ANOTHER SMALL PAN, HEAT CREAM TO SIMMER & KEEP HOT. WHEN SUGAR IS MELTED & AMBER, SLOWLY POUR IN HOT CREAM, WHISKING BRISKLY OVER LOW HEAT UNTIL SAUCE IS WELL BLENDED & RICH IN COLOR. POUR INTO A SMALL HEATED PITCHER & SERVE WARM OVER CHILLED SNOW CLOUDS. ♥

"Forth to the wood did merry men go, to gather in the mistletoe." ♥   ♥   ♥   Sir Walter Scott

KIWI·ICE

Serves Four

Light, fresh and very pretty ~ looks especially nice served in sparkly clear glass ~ bowls or sherbet glasses. ♥

4 Kiwi fruit (reserve a perfect slice for each serving.)
5 Tbsp. fresh lemon or lime juice
¼ Tbsp. grated rind
1 c. water
½ c. sugar
½ c. light corn syrup

Pureé fruit, juice and rind in blender. Cook water, sugar and corn syrup until sugar dissolves. Mix it all to~ gether and pour into a shallow pan. Put it in the freezer for 1½ hours. Take it out & beat it till light and fluffy~ Then back to the freezer for at least 2 hours more. Garnish with slices of fresh fruit. Another garnish idea would be fresh mint sprigs or pineapple slices. ♥

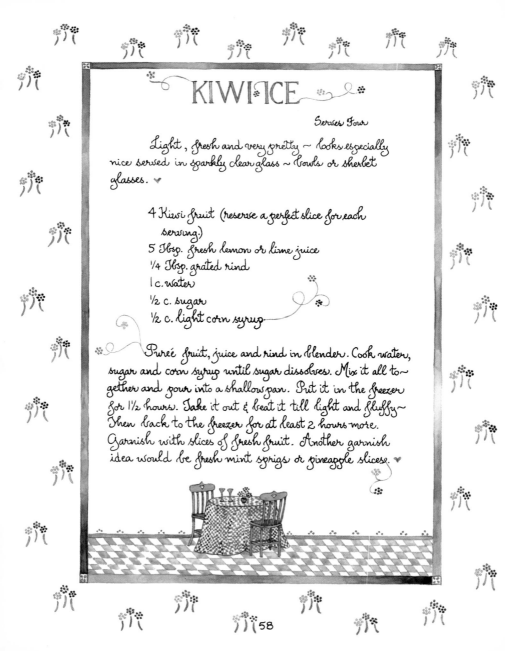

Orange Ice

Serves Four

Delicious and refreshing on its own, but for gorgeous color & more sophistication try it with Raspberry Sauce (p.43). ♥

3 c. fresh orange juice
½ c. sugar
½ c. lemon juice
grated rind of 2 oranges

Bring orange juice to boil. Stir in sugar till dissolved. Cool. Add lemon juice & rind. Freeze in hand-cranked or electric ice cream maker. You can also freeze it in a metal bowl, stirring every so often. Ices are best when served slightly mushy—not frozen stiff. ♥

Tip: The wonderful Donvier ice cream maker makes ice cream & ices in minutes with no electricity & no fuss. Get one. ♥

BOURBON BALLS

Makes about 60

A delicious holiday candy. ♥

1 box powdered sugar, plus ⅓ c.	4 oz. unsweetened chocolate
1 stick butter, softened	1 oz. paraffin wax, grated
⅓ c. bourbon	1 box toothpicks

Sift 1 box powdered sugar over butter & cream together thoroughly. Stir in bourbon & put into freezer 5 min. Sift the ⅓ c. powdered sugar onto plate. Roll sugar mixture into 1" balls, then in powdered sugar. Place them onto cookie sheet & into freezer for 15 min. Stick a toothpick into each ball. Melt chocolate & paraffin together. Working quickly, dip each ball in chocolate; place on wax paper on cookie sheet. Remove picks. Reheat chocolate, then dribble a bit more on each candy to cover toothpick hole. Put them back in freezer 5 more min. Store in covered container in refrigerator. ♥

"Lost, yesterday, somewhere between sunrise
and sunset, two golden hours, each set
with sixty diamond minutes. No reward is
offered, for they are gone forever."
♥ Horace Mann

ALMOND BRITTLE

This makes a perfect candy for gift giving—especially good for mailing. But it comes with a warning: make it, get it packed, & get it OUT of the house. Sometimes I let it sit out cooling too long & somehow it's GONE before I get it sent. (DON'T LOOK AT ME ☺) ♥

You will need a candy thermometer for this.
2 c. sugar
1 lb. unsalted (sweet) butter
¼ c. water
10 oz. sliced almonds
8 oz. unsweetened chocolate

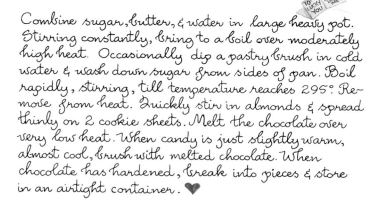

Combine sugar, butter, & water in large heavy pot. Stirring constantly, bring to a boil over moderately high heat. Occasionally dip a pastry brush in cold water & wash down sugar from sides of pan. Boil rapidly, stirring, till temperature reaches 295°. Remove from heat. Quickly stir in almonds & spread thinly on 2 cookie sheets. Melt the chocolate over very low heat. When candy is just slightly warm, almost cool, brush with melted chocolate. When chocolate has hardened, break into pieces & store in an airtight container. ♥

"Never eat more than you can lift."
Miss Piggy

FOOD & LOVE

I remember my very first chocolate eclair. I was about 5 years old & I was spending the day with my grandma. We were all dressed up & she took me downtown to a big department store that smelled like perfume. She bought me a pair of red leather shoes with a strap across the top & three little teardrop cutouts over the toe. I thought nothing could be better than this but afterwards she took me into a cake & pastry-filled bakery where everything seemed to be covered in whipped cream & chocolate. We sat in a booth in the window & my eclair was served on a plate with its own lace doily. The tender biscuit, filled with rich cream & covered in chocolate, melted in my mouth. I never tasted anything like it — it was wonderful, so, so delicious — I think I saw stars. I looked with new respect & wonder at my grandma, keeper of the keys, mystery woman, knower of all things fantastic.

Index

641.86
BRANCH

Branch, Susan.
Sweets to the sweet.

$11.45